SIGN LANGUAGE FOR BABIES BOOK

Children's Reading & Writing Education Books

All Rights reserved. No part of this book may be reproduced or used in any way or form or by any means whether electronic or mechanical, this means that you cannot record or photocopy any material ideas or tips that are provided in this book

Copyright 2016

Hand Sign Language

Bb

B is for Ball.

Ee

E is for Egg.

www.ingramcontent.com/pod-product-compliance
Lightning Source LLC
LaVergne TN
LVHW082254070426
835507LV00037B/2289